MW00952391

Legends of Rock & Roll

The Everly Brothers

An unauthorized fan tribute

By: James Hoag

"Legends of Rock & Roll – The Everly Brothers" Copyright 2011 James Hoag. All rights reserved. Manufactured in the United States of America. No parts of this book may be reproduced in any form or by any electronic or mechanical means including information storage and retrieval systems without written permission from the publisher. The only exception is for a reviewer. A reviewer may quote brief passages in a review. Published by www.number1project.com Monument Marketing Publishing LTD., 53 Hanover Dr., Orem, Utah 84058

Paperback Edition

Manufactured in the United States of America

Other Paperbacks by James Hoag

Here is a list of paperback editions that are currently available on Amazon. This list will expand as time goes by:

Legends of Rock & Roll Volume 1 - The Fifties

Legends of Rock & Roll Volume 2 - The Sixties

Legends of Rock & Roll Volume 3 - The Seventies

Legends of Rock & Roll

The Beatles
John Lennon
Paul McCartney
George Harrison
Ringo Starr
Neil Diamond
Queen
Eagles
Bruce Springsteen

Legends of Country Music

Reba McEntire
Willie Nelson
Johnny Cash
George Jones
Merle Haggard
Garth Brooks
(Available at Amazon.com)

TABLE OF CONTENTS

INTRODUCTION

When I was a boy in High School, the Everly Brothers were one of my favorite groups. Like most teenagers in those days, rock and roll was the center of my life, and the Everly Brothers were at the center of that movement; at least for me. The Everly Brothers were different because the kids liked them and so did their parents. Most parents in those days hated Rock and Roll, but the Everly Brothers were mellow enough that my Mom, at least, liked them, too.

I remember when you could go into a record store and actually play a record. They were 45 rpm in those days, (the record with the big hole in the middle). The store had little rooms that were like telephone booths. You could take the record into the booth and listen to it on a turntable, something that doesn't happen anymore.

When "All I Have to Do Is Dream" came out in 1958, I listened to it in the record store and bought it immediately. It has since become one of my all-time favorite songs. This is the kind of song that you would put on a desert island list. You know the kind of list I mean, if I could take a hundred records to a desert island, which ones would I take? "All I Have to Do Is Dream" would definitely be on that list for me. I took it home and immediately called my girlfriend. We were not going steady (yet), but we both had a love of music and so I played the song on a little 45 rpm turntable I had. I held the receiver of the phone up to the speaker of the record player. She thought it was a great song. It was especially great dancing with her to "All I Have to Do Is Dream" at the next school dance. That song eventually became a number one song for the Everly Brothers.

But I'm getting ahead of myself. This book is about the Everly Brothers so let's get into their lives and music.

1-BEFORE FAME

Don and Phil Everly are the sons of Ike and Margaret Everly. They were a musical family right from the beginning. Ike was born in Ohio County, Kentucky, but later moved to Muhlenberg County. This is coal country, and Ike worked in the mines until about 1932 when he decided to make a change and try show business. His first job was for the radio station WGBS in Muhlenberg County, KY, where he played old-time country guitar. The sound of the Everly Brothers was greatly influenced by this music.

After Margaret and Ike were married, they started playing music full time, having a little family band called "The Everly Family." They played mostly at various radio stations around Kentucky and Iowa. Ike played the guitar and Margaret played the bass fiddle.

Ike was one of the inventors of the "thumb" technique of playing the guitar. Merle Travis also perfected the technique. A fountain was constructed in Drakesboro, KY called "The Four Legends Fountain" which honors Merle Travis, Mose Rager, Ike Everly, and Kennedy Jones. All four have ties to this area of Kentucky. That fountain is still there to this day.

Isaac Donald Everly is the older of the two brothers and was born in Central City, Kentucky, on February 1, 1937. Soon after Don was born, Ike decided to move to Chicago to see if he could make a better living there. Ike worked road shows and night clubs, and it was while they were in Chicago that Phil was born on January 19, 1939. They worked for WLS (a Chicago radio station) at the same time Red Foley and George Gobel were there.

After Phil was born, Ike decided he wanted to raise the boys in a healthier environment, so they moved to Iowa. In the fall of 1944, Ike and his 2 brothers (called A Cowboy Trio) started playing at radio station KAGL in Waterloo, Iowa.

They stayed there about a year and then moved to south-western Iowa. There, they played at radio station KMA in Council Bluffs, Iowa. All this time, little Don was getting better and better at singing and playing the guitar.

Don started playing with them on a Saturday show in 1945. He was seven years old. Soon, he was so popular that it became Don's show.

Phil was too little to play, so he would tell jokes. His dad would tell him a joke at home, and he would repeat it on the air.

Phil would say: "Dad, I've done a good deed today."

Ike would answer: "Fine, Phil. What did you do?"

Phil: "You're going to be proud of me because I kept two boys from fighting."

Ike: "And who were they?"

Phil: "Well, it was me and another boy, and I ran."

He never made a mistake and the audience loved it.

They were soon rehearsing together. There were 19 different acts performing on KMA, so they got together to put on a show in Council Bluffs, Iowa called the Corn Belt Jamboree. Don was part of the show. It was said later that of all the acts playing on the station at the time, little Don Everly was the most popular.

They started paying Don $5 for each show. He was seven at the time and Phil was five. Don took the money home and divided it with his brother. It wasn't long before Phil joined the family band. On the air, they called them "Little Donnie" and "Little Boy Phil."

The family had a home recording machine. Don and Phil would stop playing outside and come in to join the family in a musical number. They rehearsed until they thought they were ready. Ike then took the recording to the local radio station to be played. The recording of Don and Phil singing together actually was played on the radio when they were probably about 7 and 9. No mention is made of what the song was, but their careers were starting.

A typical morning in the life of the brothers went like this: Get up and get ready for a 6:00 a.m. show on the radio. After the show, go home and eat breakfast and then go to school. They never missed school.

When they toured as a family it was always in the summer, so Don and Phil would not miss any school. Don graduated on time after finishing high school. Phil finished by taking correspondence courses because by the time he was in high school, they were pop stars and traveling and playing their music.

As reported in a 1958 interview with Ike Everly, he said that his wife Margaret had commented that, "It's getting good now. It just can't miss. Don and Phil are getting better every day. They are going to be great stars someday."

She was right.

In 1953, they moved to Knoxville, Tennessee, and Don and Phil gradually became better than their Dad. They sang mostly gospel and country western of the time, but Don and Phil wanted something more. Phil mentioned,

"I'd like to sing something with more of a beat."

One of their sponsors called the boys "bobby-soxers."

Things were not always good for the Everly family. Both Ike and Margaret had to train for other jobs because the music just wasn't supporting them. Radio stations found out that they could just hire one person to play records so why pay for a whole band to do it live? The jobs became fewer, and money became tight. Ike went to school and became a barber. Margaret became a beautician. They scraped by and were able to pay the bills, but times were hard.

The summer after Don graduated from high school, they were laid off and things got really desperate.

Ike knew that Chet Atkins lived in Nashville. He was a good friend of Ike's and so the two got together. Ike introduced Atkins to Don and Phil and told him he thought the boys had talent and asked if he would help them. Chet Atkins said he knew just about everyone in the music business and said to have them come to Nashville.

Chet Atkins took back to Nashville a song called "Thou Shall Not Steal" which Don had written. In 1954, Kitty Wells recorded it, and it was a fairly big hit, peaking at number 14 on the Country Charts. Don's first royalty check was for $600; that was big money in those days.

Margaret and the boys moved to Nashville.

Before long, Atkins set them up with a recording session at Columbia Records. They recorded two songs: "The Sun Keeps Shining" and "Loving Me." Neither Mom nor Dad thought they were very good. They thought the boys could do much better. Sure enough, when Columbia released the record, it didn't sell. That was the end of their very short career with Columbia Records.

2-"BYE, BYE LOVE"

Chet Atkins was friends with Wesley Rose of Acuff-Rose Music Publishers. Rose was impressed with the boys and told them that if they signed as song writers, he could get them a recording contract.

Through Rose, they got the attention of Archie Bleyer, who was then president of Cadence Records. He booked the boys for a recording session. Their first recording session with Cadence was in March of 1957.

Don and Phil had met with song writers Boudleaux and Felice Bryant, a husband wife team who penned many popular country and pop songs in the fifties. They showed Don and Phil their latest creation called "Bye, Bye Love." They had peddled it to as many as 30 performers in the Nashville area, and all had turned it down. The boys liked the song and so this was the first record Don and Phil recorded on the Cadence label. The flip side was a song called "I Wonder If I Care as Much" which was written by the brothers. The guys made $64 for recording that first song.

Bleyer announced the Everly Brothers first single with Cadence by buying a full page ad in *Billboard* magazine. In its April 20th, 1957 issue *Billboard* proclaimed,

"The Tennessee teenagers have a distinctive, appealing sound and could click big in the Pop as well as C&W fields."

At the time, country music was in a slump as rock and roll (led by people like Elvis Presley, Chuck Berry, and Little Richard) was taking over the country. As a boy, I lived in Michigan, which is not exactly the heart of country music, so I had no clue as to what was happening in the music world. All I knew was when I turned on the radio, I liked what I heard. I especially liked the harmonies of the Everlys. I couldn't have told you the technical definitions of what they sang. I just knew I liked it.

"Bye, Bye Love" hit the charts running and began to climb. It eventually sold a million copies and peaked at #2 on the Billboard charts. It didn't hurt that Don had added a "Bo Diddley" beat to the song. Back in the fifties, *Billboard* magazine had a "Best Seller" list, a "Top 100" list and among others, a "Jukebox" list. "Bye, Bye Love" reached #2 on the Best Seller list, #2 on the Top 100 list, and #9 on the Jukebox list. The two songs that kept them from the number one spot were Elvis Presley's "Teddy Bear" and Pat Boone's "Love Letters in the Sand." It did hit #1 on the Country charts where it stayed for 7 weeks. The Everly Brothers were on their way.

The Everlys were putting country music back into the mainstream. They even appeared on the Grand Ole Opry in Nashville on May 11, 1957. They sang "Bye, Bye Love" and brought the house down. The applause was so great that Roy Acuff (who was hosting) called them back to take another bow. That night, they were the first act to play the Opry that used drums. It had never been done before.

3-"WAKE UP, LITTLE SUSIE"

They quickly followed up with "Wake Up, Little Susie" which was also written by the Bryants. When you heard the opening guitar, you knew immediately what song was coming. The flip side was "Maybe Tomorrow," written by The Everlys. "Wake Up, Little Susie" was not without its controversy. I remember when it first came out; some parents wouldn't let their kids listen to it. They thought it was too risqué (remember, this was the Fifties.) The story is about a boy and girl who fall asleep during a drive-in movie and wake up in the car in the middle of the night. Wake up little Susie, we got to go home. Our reputation is shot. Some radio stations thought it was a little over the line and refused to play it.

That didn't stop the record from being their second million best seller, and their first number one. It peaked at #1 on the Best Seller chart and Top 100 chart on October 14 and stayed there for four weeks. It was their first record released with a picture sleeve. It also peaked at #1 on the Country chart where it stayed for 8 weeks.

Next the boys were asked to participate in a 78-city tour of one-nighters called "The Biggest Show of Stars for 1957." Of course the tour didn't come near me. I would have killed to see a show like that. Besides the Everlys also appearing were some of the greats of the time who later became legends of Rock and Roll. There was Buddy Knox ("Party Doll"), The Drifters, Chuck Berry ("School Day"), Paul Anka ("Diana"), The Crickets ("That'll Be the Day" - Buddy Holly hadn't taken center stage yet), Eddie Cochran ("Sittin' in the Balcony"), LaVern Baker ("Jim Dandy"), Fats Domino ("Blueberry Hill"), Frankie Lymon ("Why Do Fools Fall in Love"), Clyde McPhatter ("Treasure of Love") and the Paul Williams Orchestra.

James Hoag

4-"ALL I HAVE TO DO IS DREAM"

"All I Have to Do Is Dream" was recorded on Mar 6, 1958. Besides being my favorite song of the Everlys, it is probably their best known song. Of course, that might depend on who you talk to. The song was introduced on Dick Clark's American Bandstand in which Dick said, "This is their next number one song." And it was. It was at the top of the pop charts for five weeks.

After three big selling records, it was time for an album. Their first album, the self-titled *The Everly Brothers,* was released in April of 1958 and included the songs they had previously released as singles, plus others including "This Little Girl of Mine" also done by Ray Charles, "Should I Tell Him?" and "Live I Have to Live," written by Don and Phil, "Sun Keeps Shining" and "Keep a Lovin' Me" written by Don. "Live I Have to Live" was first recorded by Justin Tubb who had a short career in the fifties. Justin was the son the famous country singer Ernest Tubb.

From 1957 until 1959, the boys had six top 10 records on the country charts and seven top 10s on the pop chart, a feat no one else had ever done.

On June 30, 1957, the Everly Brothers appeared on *The Ed Sullivan Show.* Sullivan was one of the highest ranking shows on TV in the fifties, and this would be a big boost to their career. They sang "Bye, Bye Love" which was their big hit of the year.

In 1958, they recorded "Claudette" which was written by Roy Orbison in honor of his wife.

In 1961, "Ebony Eyes" which hit number eight on the pop charts was the last song to make the country charts, peaking at number 25. It would be twenty-three years before they hit the country charts again.

By 1962, the Everlys had earned over $35 million dollars from record sales. They were the stars of the Cadence label. They were hitting the charts in the United States and in the United Kingdom. Under Cadence, they recorded two albums and 10 singles, most of them written by the Bryants.

Don and Phil toured with Buddy Holly during 1957 and 1958. Holly was killed in the famous plane crash in February of 1959. Phil acted as a pallbearer at Buddy Holly's funeral. Don was too distraught and didn't attend the funeral. It was said that the Everlys were responsible for Holly and the Crickets changing their look from Levi's and T-shirts to a sharper Ivy League suit look.

The three years at Cadence proved that The Everly Brothers were star material, the stuff of which legends are made. The Everlys sang to the kids of the day, to the tortures of young love and breakups. They sang with a yearning and with compelling melodies. The kids could relate to everything they sang. I know they sang to me. They were really the first to combine country music and pop together which made them both accessible without sacrificing any power or beauty.

They were not as raw as some of the artists of the day, like Jerry Lee Lewis and Little Richard, but they could still rock when they wanted. With a team like Archie Bleyer, Chet Atkins, and the Bryant's, how could they go wrong?

5-THE WARNER BROTHER YEARS

But, it did go wrong. Shortly after signing with Warner Brothers, the duo had a falling out with their manager Wesley Rose. Unfortunately, he also controlled the Acuff-Rose Music Publishing Company. This meant that, for several years in the 1960's, the Everlys could not get access to the Bryants and even some of their own work which they had written was locked out for them. This lasted until 1964.

The Everlys stayed with Cadence for three years and then, in 1960, signed what was reported to be a 10-year, multi-million dollar contract with Warner Brothers. They were to stay with Warner Brothers for the next ten years.

In 1960, Don and Phil wrote "Cathy's Clown" which was their first number 1 on the Warner label. It eventually sold 8 million copies, which made it the guy's biggest selling record of their career. It was also the first record Warner Brothers released in the United Kingdom.

Other Warner Brothers hits were: "So Sad (To Watch Good Love Go Bad)" (1960, #7), "Walk Right Back" (1961, #7), "Crying In The Rain" (1962, #6), and "That's Old Fashioned" (1962, #9, their last Top 10 hit).

Cadence had some records in the vault that they had not yet released, so they released them. The two biggest of these were "When Will I Be Loved" (written by Phil) (#8) and "Like Strangers" (#22). That was the end for Cadence. They never cracked the Top 40 again on the Cadence label.

By 1964, the British Invasion was well under way. While the Everlys were still charting in England (rather ironic, I think), Canada and Australia, their popularity in the United States was suffering, so they ended up recording other people's work. The quality started sliding downward and along with it, their positions in the charts.

6-THE MARINES

The last nail in the coffin was being called to serve in the military. The Vietnam War was just getting started, the draft was in effect, and so to keep from being drafted, the guys enlisted in the U.S. Marines Reserves. On November 21, 1961, Don and Phil joined the Marine Corp Reserves for six months. They served six months during which time no new music was being produced. They went through boot camp in San Diego and then spent their tour of duty at Camp Pendleton, California. The only highlight of that six month period was another appearance on *The Ed Sullivan Show* during a time when they were on leave. They sang "Jezebel" and "Crying in the Rain."

While still in the Marines, on February 13, 1962, Don married movie starlet Venetia Stevenson in the chapel at Camp Pendleton. Don was wearing his dress uniform.

After their tour in the Marines, Don and Phil tried to pick up where they had left off but couldn't quite connect with an audience. Between 1963 and 1970, they recorded another 27 singles (See discography) but only three of them cracked the Top 100 and only two of those made the Top 40: "Gone, Gone, Gone" (1964, #31) and "Bowling Green" (1967, #40).

Their personal lives began to unravel as well.

They both became addicted to speed for a while, and Don almost died of an overdose in 1962.

Don also started taking Ritalin which just made things worse. Don's addiction lasted for three years, and he was eventually hospitalized after a nervous breakdown. The guys were still very popular in Great Britain and about this time, they started a United Kingdom tour. During this tour, Don found that he could not go on, so he left the tour and returned to the states, while their bass player, Joey Page, took his place on stage. Phil had to finish the tour alone.

7-THE BRITISH INVASION

When the Beatles hit the scene, everything changed. It's ironic that the Beatles owe much of what they wrote to influences of other Fifties groups like the Everly Brothers, but it was the advent of the Beatles that put many of these bands out of business. The music world had changed forever.

The Everlys recorded an album called *Two Yanks in England* especially for their British fans. The record was recorded in England and The Hollies, a major British group, sang with them on the album. The Hollies actually wrote many of the songs on the album. This album is still in print.

One of the most respected albums they did during the sixties was *Roots*, which was fairly ignored by the public but got great critical acclaim. *Roots* was intended to take them back to their country days. It is considered one of the first country rock albums. It contains parts of recordings which they made back in the days when they were children, and they played on the radio with their parents. This is an album that a devoted fan of The Everly Brothers must have. This album is also still available.

The work they did during the mid-sixties was well received by the critics and those who got the chance to hear the albums were favorably impressed. Their work was compared to the Beatles and the Byrds. However, people just did not buy enough of them to get them back on the charts.

They pushed on. They continued to record, and they continued to tour, but it was not the same. Their contract with Warner Brothers expired in 1970, and Warner did not renew it. They spent some time doing TV. During the summer of 1970, they replaced Johnny Cash on his show. The show was called *Johnny Cash Presents The Everly*

Brothers, but that didn't get very good ratings, either. The one highlight of the show was the night Don and Phil decided to bring their father, Ike, out of retirement to perform with them before a national audience.

8-BREAKING UP

After Warner Brothers let them go, they signed with RCA, but nothing would ever be the same. They toured, they recorded some albums, but they were having serious personal problems. In the summer of 1973, it all came to a head. During a concert at Knott's Berry Farm in California, during the second of three scheduled shows, the manager come on stage and stopped the show. He told the audience that Don was performing sloppily. Phil, very upset, smashed his guitar on the stage and walked off. It was the end of the Everly Brothers (at least for a while.)

Don remarked, "The Everly Brothers died 10 years ago."

9-THE SOLO YEARS

They spent the next 10 years doing solo work. This primarily had the effect of proving to the public just how much each brother needed the other to sound their best.

Don continued to write and recorded some solo albums on labels Ode and Hickory, as did Phil. A song that Phil had written back in 1960, "When Will I Be Loved", (and hit the top 10 for the Everlys) was covered by Linda Ronstadt and became a big hit for her. Phil sang harmony on that record. Phil hosted a radio show in the seventies that he called *In Session*.

Don formed a band called "The Dead Cowboys". He hit the country charts in 1976 with "Yesterday Just Passed My Way Again" (#50), again in 1977 with "Since You Broke My Heart" (#84) and "Brother Juke-box" (#96). In 1991, Mark Chesnutt had a number one hit with "Brother Juke-Box"

Phil recorded a version of "The Air That I Breathe", which was a big hit by the Hollies about a year later. In 1983, Phil recorded an album which got good reviews in England and had several admirers, including Mark Knopler. He also charted on the country charts with "Dare to Dream Again" (1980, #63), "Sweet Southern Love" (1981, #52), and "Who's Gonna Keep Me Warm" (1983 #37).

There were other things which kept them busy. Phil sang backup for Warren Zevon on two songs from the self-titled "Warren Zevon" album and Don recorded a duet with Emmylou Harris in 1979. The song was "Every Time You Leave" on her *Blue Kentucky Girl* album. Phil wrote "Don't Say You Don't Love Me No More" which appeared in the Clint Eastwood movie *Every Which Way But Loose* (1978). He performed it with Sondra Locke who was a co-star in the movie. Eastwood must have liked Phil because he also wrote "One Too Many

Women In Your Life" for the follow-up movie *Any Which Way You Can* (1980). He appears in the movie playing behind Sondra Locke as she sings the song. Phil recorded a self-titled album *Phil Everly* which was fairly successful in the United Kingdom. One track, "She Means Nothing To Me" featuring Cliff Richards was a Top 10 song in England.

10-THE REUNION

On September 23, 1983, after their father's funeral, Don and Phil finally made peace with each other. They reunited for the first time in over ten years. They agreed to do a reunion concert at Royal Albert Hall in London. It was wonderful. I saw it on TV and was thrilled to hear the harmonies again. It was released on vinyl as a two-record set and several different versions of a DVD of the concert have been released. If you watch the DVD, you'll realize that it seems like they were never gone. They just look a little older. Picking right up where they left off, their voices at age 44 and 46 still sounded the same. The harmonies were still there.

The band of the Albert Hall concert included Albert Lee (who was also musical director for the concert), Pete Wingfield on the piano, plus three members of Cliff Richard's band: Graham Jarvis on the drums, Mark Griffiths on bass, and Martin Jenner on pedal steel guitar. They sang all of their hits and included a medley of "Devoted to You/Ebony Eyes/Love Hurts."

The Everly Brothers were inducted in the Rock and Roll Hall of Fame in 1986. This was the first year of the Hall of Fame, so they were among the first to be inducted. They were introduced by Neil Young, who mentioned that every group he had ever been a member of had tried and failed to copy the Everly Brothers.

In 1989, on his Cinemax Special, Chet Atkins said of the brothers, "They simply changed music for the whole world."

The Bee Gees admitted that they sang in the style of the Everlys, they just added a third harmony. If you listen to the Bee Gee's hit "New York Mining Disaster," you can hear the Everly style.

In the years after the reunion, they recorded three albums which have become significant. *EB84,* produced by Dave Edmunds, was released in 1984, obviously. The main thing of significance about this album was that it contained the song "On the Wings of a Nightingale" which was written for them by Paul McCartney. It charted on the country charts but didn't make the pop Top 40.

In 1986, they recorded *Born Yesterday* which was selected by *Time Magazine* as one of the top ten pop albums of the year. It was not, however, a commercial success. In 1989, *Some Hearts* was released, and it turned out that this was to be their last original album. This was their fifth decade of recording.

11-UP TO THE PRESENT

Music definitely runs in the Everly Family. Don's son Edan would often tour with them and join them on stage and sing along.

Don and Phil also joined Paul Simon on the title track of his award-winning album *Graceland*.

In 1994, Rhino Records issued a 4-CD 103-song set of most of their records. The set spans the entire recording career of Don and Phil. Forty of the tracks had never been on CD before, and twelve were in stereo for the first time.

In February of 1997, the brothers received a Lifetime Achievement Award from The Recording Academy. The list of people who have received this is a who's who of American and British music. It includes Bob Dylan, Stevie Wonder, Fats Domino, Barbra Streisand, Paul McCartney, The Rolling Stones, and their old friend Chet Atkins.

In 2003, the boys were still touring. They had a repertoire of 26 songs which they sang frequently. They had had sales of 40 million records over their career. Simon and Garfunkel, who themselves had been solo for many years after separating in the early seventies, came back with a reunion tour called "Old Friends" during 2003 and 2004. They asked the Everlys to perform with them. Now, usually, if you perform with a big headlining act, you are the opening act, and the big name comes on after. Simon and Garfunkel loved the Everlys so much that they opened the show, did a few numbers, and then had Don and Phil come out for a short show in the middle of the concert. Then Simon and Garfunkel came on and finished the concert.

My wife and I saw that concert in Salt Lake City. It was the first and only time I have ever seen the Everly Brothers in person. They did only three songs right in the middle and then it went back to Simon and Garfunkel. They definitely left us wanting more. It was a wonderful concert, one of the highlights of my life. Simon and Garfunkel were great but what I remember most about the concert was those three songs that the Everlys did. Now, I can die happy.

12-THE PASSING OF PHIL EVERLY

(Author's note): This was added to the book in 2016 about two years after Phil Everly passed away.

On January 3, 2014, Phil died of lung disease. Phil had been a heavy smoker most of his life and even though he had tried to quit several times, the damage had been done. He was diagnosed with chronic obstructive pulmonary disease (COPD) in 2011 His last public appearance was in 2011 when he attended the induction of Buddy Holly into the Hollywood Star Walk of Fame. When he tried to address the crowd, he found himself getting out of breath and having to stop several times before he could continue and finish his remarks.

During his final years, he carried an oxygen tank with him everywhere he went, so he could breathe. Things went from bad to worse and finally, he entered Providence Saint Joseph Medical Center in Burbank, California, where he died on January 3. He was seventy-four years old.

13-LEGACY OF THE EVERLY BROTHERS

The Everly Brothers have impacted many of the greatest names of Rock and Roll. The Beatles declare they owe much to the brothers. The Beach Boys and Simon and Garfunkel also owe much of their success to The Everly Brothers.

The Beatles based the arrangement for "Please Please Me" upon "Cathy's Clown."

Keith Richards of the Rolling Stones called Don Everly, "One of the finest rhythm players."

The Kingston Trio recorded a song for their *String Along* Album called "Everglades." In it, they paid tribute to the Everlys. Some of the lyrics go like this:

"But he better keep movin' and don't stand still. If the 'skeeters don't get you then the 'gaters will. Runnin' like a dog through the Everglades. (Last line - Skippin' like a frog through the slimy bog. Runnin' through the trees from the Everlys.")

Bob Dylan once said, regarding Don and Phil, "We owe these guys everything. They started it all."

What more do I need to say?

ABOUT THE AUTHOR

James Hoag has always been a big fan of Rock & Roll. Most people graduate from high school and then proceed to "grow up" and go on to more adult types of music. James got stuck at about age 18 and has been an avid fan of popular music ever since. His favorite music is from the Fifties, the origin of Rock & Roll and which was the era in which James grew up. But he likes almost all types of popular music including country music.

After working his entire life as a computer programmer, he is now retired and he decided to share his love of the music and of the performers by writing books that discuss the life and music of the various people who have meant so much to him over the years.

He calls each book a "love letter" to the stars that have enriched our lives so much. These people are truly Legends.

SELECTED DISCOGRAPHY

The Everly Brothers have released 21 studio albums, 3 live albums, and 75 singles.

ALBUMS

1958 "The Everly Brothers" Cadence

1959 "Songs Our Daddy Taught Us" Cadence

1960 "It's Everly Time" Warner Brothers

1961 "A Date with the Everly Brothers" Warner Brothers

1961 "Both Sides of an Evening" Warner Brothers

1962 "Instant Party!" Warner Brothers

1962 "Christmas with the Everly Brothers" Warner Brothers

1963 "The Everly Brothers Sing Great Country Hits" Warner Brothers

1964 "Gone Gone Gone" Warner Brothers

1965 "Rock & Soul" Warner Brothers

1965 "Beat & Soul" Warner Brothers

1966 "In Our Image" Warner Brothers

1966 "Two Yanks in England" Warner Brothers

1967 "The Hit Sound of the Everly Brothers" Warner Brothers

1967 "The Everly Brothers Sing" Warner Brothers

1968 "Roots" Warner Brothers

1972 "Stories We Could Tell" RCA

1973 "Pass the Chicken and Listen" RCA

1984 "EB 84" Mercury

1986 "Born Yesterday" Mercury

1988 "Some Hearts" Mercury

LIVE ALBUMS

1970 "Everly Brothers Show" Warner Bros.

1983 "The Everly Brothers Reunion Concert" Passport

1996 "Everly Brothers Live" BCI Music

SINGLES

1956 "KeepA-Lovin' Me"/"The Sun Keeps Shining" Columbia

1957 "Bye, Bye Love"/"I Wonder if I Care as Much" Cadence

1957 "Wake Up Little Susie"/"Maybe Tomorrow" Cadence

1957 "This Little Girl of Mine"/"Should We Tell Him" Cadence

1958 "All I Have to Do is Dream"/"Claudette" Cadence

1958 "Bird Dog"/"Devoted to You" Cadence

1958 "Problems"/"Love of My Life" Cadence

1959 "Rip It Up" Cadence

1959 "Take a Message to Mary"/"Poor Jenny" Cadence

1959 "(Til) I Kissed You"/"Oh What a Feeling" Cadence

1959 "Let It Be Me"/"Since You Broke My Heart" Cadence

1959 "Cathy's Clown"/"Always It's You" Warner Bros

1960 "When Will I Be Loved"/"Be-Bop-a-Lula" Cadence

1960 "So Sad"/"Lucille" Warner Bros

1960 "Like Strangers"/"Brand New Heartache" Cadence

1960 "Walk Right Back"/Ebony Eyes" Warner Bros

1960 "Temptation"/ "Stick With Me, Baby" Warner Bros

1961 "Don't Blame Me"/"Muskrat" Warner Bros

1961 "Crying in the Rain"/"I'm Not Angry" Warner Bros

1961 "That's Old Fashioned"/"How Can I Meet Her" Warner Bros

1962 "I'm Here to Get My Baby Out of Jail"/"Lightning Express" Cadence

1962 "Don't Ask Me to Be Friends"/"No One Can Make My Sunshine Smile" Warner Bros

1962 "Nancy's Minuet"/"(So It Was, So It Is) So It Always Will Be" Warner Bros

1963 "It's Been Nice Goodnight"/"I'm Afraid" Warner Bros

1963 "The Girl Sang the Blues"/"Love Her" Warner Bros

1964 "Ain't That Lovin' You, Baby"/"Hello Amy" Warner Bros

1964 "The Ferris Wheel"/"Don't Forget to Cry" Warner Bros

1964 "You're the One I Love"/"Ring Around My Rosie" Warner Bros

1964 "Gone, Gone, Gone"/"Torture" Warner Bros

1964 "You're My Girl"/"Don't Let the Whole World Know" Warner Bros

1964 "That'll Be the Day"/"Give Me a Sweetheart" Warner Bros

1965 "The Price of Love"/"It Only Costs a Dime" Warner Bros

1965 "I'll Never Get Over You"/"Follow Me" Warner Bros

1965 "Love is Strange"/"Man With Money" Warner Bros

1965 "It's All Over"/"I Used to Love Her" Warner Bros

1966 "The Dollhouse is Empty"/"Lovey Kravezit" Warner Bros

1966 "(You Got) The Power of Love"/"Leave My Girl Alone" Warner Bros

1966 "Somebody Help Me"/"Hard Hard Year" Warner Bros

1966 "Fifi the Flea"/"Like Everytime Before" Warner Bros

1966 "The Devil's Child"/"She Never Smiles Anymore" Warner Bros

1967 "Bowling Green"/"I Don't Want To Love You" Warner Bros

1967 "Mary Jane"/"Talking to the Flowers" Warner Bros

1967 "Love of the Common People"/"A Voice Within" Warner Bros

1968 "It's My Time"/"Empty Boxes" Warner Bros

1968 "Milk Train"/"Lord of the Manor" Warner Bros

1968 "T for Texas"/"I Wonder if I Care as Much" Warner Bros

1969 "I'm On My Way Home Again"/"Cuckoo Bird" Warner Bros

1969 "Carolina in My Mind"/"My Little Yellow Bird" Warner Bros

1970 "Yves"/Human Race" Warner Bros

1972 "Ridin' High"/"Stories We Could Tell" RCA

1972 "Lay It Down"/"Paradise" RCA

1973 "Not Fade Away"/"Ladies Love Outlaws" RCA

1984 "On the Wings of a Nightingale"/"Asleep" Mercury

1985 "The First in Line"/"Story of Me" Mercury

1985 "Born Yesterday"/"Don't Say Goodnight" Mercury

1986 "I Know Love"/"These Shoes" Mercury

1988 "Don't Worry Baby"/"Tequila Dreams" Capitol

Don Everly (Solo)

1970 "Tumblin' Tumbleweeds"

1974 "Warmin' Up the Band"

1976 "Yesterday Just Passed My Way Again"

1976 "Love at Last Sight"

1977 "Since You Broke My Heart"

1977 "Brother Jukebox"

1981 "Let's Put Our Hearts Together"

Phil Everly (Solo)

1973 "God Bless Older Ladies (For They Made Rock and Roll)"

1974 "Old Kentucky River"

1975 "New Old Song"

1975 "Words in Your Eyes"

1979 "Living Alone"

1979 "You Broke It"

1980 "Dare to Dream Again"

1981 "Sweet Southern Love"

1982 "Louise"

1982 "Who's Gonna Keep Me Warm"

1982 "She Means Nothing to Me" (with Cliff Richard)

1982 "Sweet Pretender"

1994 "All I Have to Do Is Dream" (with Cliff Richard)

Made in the USA
Columbia, SC
22 November 2023

26955592R00022